HOW TO BI WORLD CH PROFESSIONAL ⌐ᴧᴧᴇʀ EXPOSED!

By Stephen Gibbs

How Can You Become A Professional Wrestler?

Before you become a professional wrestler, you should understand the basic rules of the sport. Wrestling is a team sport and the objective is not only to win matches but also to entertain the audience. The audience expects good performances from the wrestlers and they must treat other wrestlers as teammates. You should be aware of how to work with other wrestlers, but you also need to practice heavy-contact moves.

A sports background in general helps

Many famous wrestlers have a sports background. While playing sports is not only beneficial for keeping fit, but it also instills positive traits in a person. In addition to developing teamwork skills, sports improve concentration and discipline. Wrestling is a demanding sport, and the experience gained from playing sports helps a person develop the skills necessary to succeed. So, if you're considering a career in professional wrestling, consider a sports background.

Wrestling

If you have a passion for wrestling, you might want to learn how to become a professional wrestler. While pursuing this dream, you will need to put in a lot of hard work. You will have to learn from top trainers and join every decent wrestling program in your area. Although this may seem like a daunting task, it will pay off when you finally make it to the big leagues. Here are some tips to make the dream of becoming a professional wrestler a reality.

Observe people. You can observe professional wrestlers to learn about their persona and character. You can ask for tips from them and learn from their mistakes. Try to make your fans laugh and post updates about upcoming matches. You can also try asking them for advice on how to become a professional wrestler. You can also take advantage of a manager who knows how to work a crowd and manage a match.

A mentor is a must. You can get a coach or mentor from someone who has already made it in the sport. It is also important to join a wrestling gym or club to develop the right kind of skills. You should be prepared to work hard for your career and devote the time required. Remember that professional wrestling is not easy, so you have to have the right mindset to succeed. You also need a team and a supportive coach.

A professional wrestler should be in top-notch shape. This means spending hours at the gym each week. Whether it is lifting weights or doing cardio exercises, you need to maintain an ample amount of muscle size and definition. You should also focus on your diet, as a professional wrestler has a unique diet that promotes muscle building, minimizes excess body fat and provides energy. You should watch other wrestlers to see what works for them.

Bodybuilding

If you are wondering how to become a professional wrestler, you've come to the right place. The most well-known bodybuilders in history are all pros in the ring, including Sting, Lex Luger, and Hulk Hogan. These legendary wrestlers mastered their craft as amateur bodybuilders and became world famous. Here are three examples of how bodybuilding made them famous:

If you've ever watched WWE, you've seen pro wrestlers work out and build massive muscles. Oftentimes, these wrestlers are also known for their sexy physiques. Brian Cage, the agile big man in pro wrestling, got into bodybuilding in his early twenties and won a bodybuilding competition at age 20. Another great example of this is Triple H. He began bodybuilding when he was just a teenager and won the Mr. Teenage New Hampshire title.

Wrestling is as much an art form as a sport, and the superhuman physiques of these wrestlers catch the public's eye and encourage people to buy tickets. In 1990, Vince McMahon urged wrestlers to build their muscles, creating the World Bodybuilding Federation (WBF) - a group that would later go on to produce Mr. Olympia winners.

A prospective pro wrestler can begin building his or her body on their own, but there are pitfalls. A better option is to hire a personal trainer who can guide you through the process. There are several professional wrestling schools, including those run by former pro wrestlers, which focus on training professional wrestlers. Wrestling schools teach fundamental wrestling moves and specific elements that can be used in the ring.

Attending Wrestling schools

If you want to become a professional wrestler, there are many different ways to go about it. While you might want to be famous and rich, it will take work and experience to make it in the business. Nevertheless, you can achieve your goal with hard work and dedication. Below are some tips that will help you on your way to becoming a professional wrestler. Become an athlete by training hard and attending wrestling schools to become a professional wrestler.

Wrestling is a very competitive sport, and you should start training at an early age. While there are many people in the WWE who get their big break, there are only a handful who succeed. Therefore, you should start training while you're still young and in good physical shape. There are also some specialized training schools and trainers who will help you achieve your dreams of becoming a professional wrestler.

In order to excel in this sport, you should attend wrestling schools to learn the basics of the sport. There are a lot of advantages of going to such an institution, including the practical and theoretical aspects of the sport. There is also a plagiarism checker available for free. EduBirdie is well-known in the academic arena. Wrestling schools will also teach you about the proper way to write a resume.

You should be at least 18 years old to attend this school. The world famous Reality of Wrestling is also one of the best places to attend a wrestling school. This school is run by legendary wrestler Booker T, who won numerous world championships. Students will learn the correct wrestling techniques and build the best storyline possible. If you're serious about pursuing a career in professional wrestling, it is important to get the right training to become the best professional wrestler possible.

Team work

A key element in the process of becoming a professional wrestler is teamwork. As a professional wrestler, you are expected to work together as a team and be a good example for your teammates. Teamwork is essential to a successful wrestling career, and is often overlooked. According to Troy Nickerson, head wrestling coach at the University of Northern Colorado, wrestling isn't just about winning matches. It is also about entertaining an audience. In order to impress the crowd, you must work together with other wrestlers and view your opponents as teammates. This means you have to practice teamwork as well as heavy-contact moves.

How Much Does It Cost To Become a Professional Wrestler?

If you've ever wondered how much it costs to become a professional wrestler, you aren't alone. The financial commitment for the sport isn't nearly as complex as it seems. Here are some of the common expenses you will face as you become a professional wrestler. While some training methods are free, others require a membership to access the training materials. A typical session at a professional wrestling school will cost between $20 and $30.

What's the financial commitment to wrestling?

Becoming a professional wrestler requires substantial financial investment. You'll also need to travel a lot to reach your performances. If you're not used to sleeping in your own bed, you'll need to stay in hotels or friends' houses to stay overnight. A yearlong program at a specialized wrestling school may cost anywhere from $1000 to $5,000.

To become a professional wrestler is a long and challenging career. Wrestling promotion companies need to obtain a business license and become tax-paying entities. In addition to paying for training, you must pay for costumes, props, and make-up, which isn't cheap. Fortunately, YouTube has made this task much easier. In addition to training, you'll also need to purchase equipment to train at home.

The pro wrestling industry uses campaigns and products to reach young children, as well as adults. It is important to note that pro wrestling targets the vulnerable segment of the population, and its products are designed to attract young adult males. This demographic is particularly vulnerable to marketing, and wrestling promotes potentially harmful products. And since children are more susceptible to absorbing messages from televised media, these messages have a significant impact on their social development.

While becoming a professional wrestler is not for everyone, it is a lucrative profession that offers many rewards. If you have a name and brand value, you could charge up to a few thousand dollars per appearance. Wrestlers don't advertise their fees, but a few have been reported to charge between $2,500 and $5,000 per show. Top talent such as Brock Lesnar and John Cena earn millions of dollars a year.

Common expenses to Become a Professional Wrestler

While it may seem like becoming a professional wrestler is difficult, the truth is that it isn't as complicated as it seems. There are many expenses involved, including tuition for wrestling school. Most students pay between $2,300 and $3,500 a year for classes, but the price of a program can be much lower. The cost of a first class may be as little as $20, while the cost of additional training may be between $30 and $75 per session.

Wrestling requires a lot of gear to begin. Singlets and headgear are two of the major expenses. The fees for these items vary depending on the brand and customization. Some gear is versatile and can be used for multiple seasons. In addition, wrestling shows often require traveling for eight hours or more. Since traveling can be a hassle, you'll likely have to stay in hotels or at friends' houses while you're away.

In order to become a professional wrestler, students must spend a lot of time learning the art of wrestling. While it is an extremely beneficial sport that trains the mind and body, it can also be very expensive. While you can find classes for less money on YouTube, it is important to select a reputable wrestling school. If you're looking to become a professional wrestler, then choosing the right school will be crucial to your success.

To succeed as a professional wrestler, you must spend years of free time learning the trade and establishing your name as a respected person. The more you practice, the better you'll become. The key to success is talent and hard work. Whether it's wrestling or other sports, talent is the winning formula. So, what are you waiting for? Get started now by reading these helpful tips. Once you've become an expert in your craft, you'll be well on your way to a lucrative and fulfilling career.

A typical salary of $12,800 per year is common for a professional wrestler, but that figure can vary greatly. Wrestlers with a name brand and a high profile can command several thousand dollars for an appearance. Most wrestlers do not advertise their fees, but some rake in more than $1 million per year. While you're earning millions per year, there are still expenses that you need to pay. A flight and lodging are typical costs.

How do you make money as a professional wrestler

If you are passionate about wrestling, you might wonder how to make money as a professional wrestler. There are several ways that fans of the sport can earn money. In addition to doing your passion justice, there are several opportunities to become a professional wrestler. All it takes is action. After all, you've been hooked for so long that you want to make money! However, before you take action, it's important to understand what is required to become a professional wrestler.

While wrestling is a profession with high salaries, you can still make money in the sport. You can earn anywhere from $25,000 to $1 million a year by participating in professional wrestling shows.

Some pro wrestlers can make millions of dollars, including superstars in the Ring of Honor. Even indie wrestlers are not guaranteed a full-time living in the industry, but many have made millions of dollars.

The best way to break into the industry as a professional wrestler is to enroll in a professional wrestling school. While there are hundreds of such schools, there are only a few that are worthwhile. You should do your homework to find the most appropriate school for you. Anarchy Championship Wrestling operates Pro Wrestling Dojo in San Antonio, Texas. Those who have had good experiences with the company run their own wrestling schools.

Wrestling is a highly lucrative career with many sources of income. The biggest names in WWE make over $1 million a year. In addition to their base salaries, these wrestlers also receive PPV bonuses, licensing deals, and other perks. The difference in income is huge. Wrestlers on average make $100,000, and the highest-paid superstars make as much as $2 million. However, despite these lucrative opportunities, you must consider that professional wrestling careers can be short-lived and the competition can be tough.

How to Become a Pro Wrestler - Training Tips

If you've always dreamed of becoming a professional wrestler, there are several ways to start training and improving your skills. Here are some of the best ways to train and become an impressive wrestler. First, find a coach or wrestle school to help you develop your skills and create a persona. Next, you'll need to join a wrestling gym or school.

Exercise a lot

While wrestling is not a sport that demands extreme strength and conditioning, the discipline requires tremendous agility. This is the reason why agility exercises such as lunges, walking toe touches, and lateral jogging are so important. You should also incorporate a variety of static stretches, such as arm circles and lateral jogging, into your regular workout. Focus on your major muscle groups and hold each stretch for at least 15 seconds.

Strength and endurance training is important for all wrestlers. The term endurance refers to the heart's ability to withstand sustained, intense exercise. You'll need to be able to maintain moderate intensity for 40 minutes. You'll also need to train to increase the muscle fibers responsible for speed, power, and endurance. You should focus on maximizing the strength and endurance of your lower body muscles, especially your legs and back.

In order to develop overall strength, you'll need to train with odd objects. Athletes often train with awkward objects, which challenge their grip, body maneuverability, and strength at odd angles. Wrestlers can benefit from training with strange objects, like bearhug carries, sandbag deadlifts, and log bicep curls. The most important area to train is your legs, back, and arms. You'll want to do 2-4 sets of six to ten reps to develop the strength in each of these areas.

Find a coach

There are many benefits to becoming a pro wrestler, and the best way to achieve your goals is to get the right training. You need to have plenty of time for training, be willing to take risks and be dedicated to your goal. Wrestling can be an extremely competitive career, and breaking into it can be difficult, but with the right training and networking, you can start your journey and reach your goal.

Finding a mentor is one of the most important aspects of becoming a professional wrestler. Your coach needs to have experience in the professional wrestling scene and can help you find promotions in the sport. The best way to learn more about the business is to get involved in events and network with other wrestlers. Wrestling is a team sport and every member is there to entertain the crowd. By working with a coach, you can learn from their mistakes and become a better wrestler.

A good coach will be able to provide you with tips and tricks on how to become a pro wrestler. Remember that professional wrestling is a long journey. You will experience injuries and bounce back afterward. Be prepared to work hard and join a wrestling gym or club in your area. A coach will help you stay motivated and help you reach your goals. If you are serious about becoming a pro wrestler, find a coach who shares your passion for the sport.

Join the wrestling school

While you may not be able to afford to join a wrestling school to become a professional wrestler, you can still pursue your dream. While you can't get rich or even make any money at first, you can become a professional wrestler and have a professional resume. It can take several years to make it into the business, but you can learn how to become a pro by joining a wrestling school.

Many people aspire to be professional wrestlers, and getting signed with the WWE is much easier than getting drafted into the NBA. After graduating from a wrestling school, you will need to make a character, order a custom costume, move to Florida, and attend shows to network with the trainers. You can also perform matches at the wrestling school and gain valuable performance experience. You will need to practice for many hours each day to be an elite wrestler.

You'll need athletic and technical skills to become a professional wrestler. You'll need to develop your own personal style as well as your presentation skills. You'll also need to abide by the wrestling code of conduct. The more you practice, the better you'll become at this game, and you'll be earning lots of money. While it's difficult to make money and gain a large following, it's worth it. You might even want to become a celebrity.

Create a persona

One of the first things you need to do if you want to become a professional wrestler is create a character or persona that you will be famous for. This persona should be unique and will have an interesting backstory. You can exaggerate your natural qualities or be someone you'd never want to meet. Whatever it is, you must make your character memorable. You can even take inspiration from other famous wrestlers for your character.

Creating a persona is as important as learning how to put on a brawl or how to hit your opponent. Wrestlers need to have a distinctive character, but some promotions fail to remember that these characters are often adored by the audience. In the NXT world, you can develop a character that combines your own personality with that of your opponents. If you're unsure of the character you'd like to become, ask a seasoned wrestler for advice.

It is easier to get signed with WWE than the NBA. To get started, you should go to a wrestling school, create a persona, order a custom costume, and start attending shows. Then, you'll be able to network with trainers and attend events to get recognized as a pro wrestler. Some wrestling schools may even hold matches for their trainees. In addition to developing a career in the ring, attending shows and networking with WWE trainers will also help you gain valuable performing experience.

Observe and copy the pros

If you want to be a pro wrestler, you have to learn a lot from the professionals. Wrestling is an art form and requires great artistic skills. Rather than trying to copy a specific move or routine, you should copy bits and pieces of the moves they use. Eventually, you'll be able to incorporate these elements into your own style. Wrestling is about entertainment, and it's important to impress the crowd.

Those who dream of becoming a pro wrestler need to develop the skills necessary for showmanship and charisma. This includes acting, public speaking, and developing one's character. This includes taking classes on personal character development. This will help you stand out from the rest of the crowd. Once you've mastered these skills, you can aim for greater heights in the sport. If you've been a fan of the pros, you can copy what they do.

Team up

Bowens and Caster are a perfect example of how to team up when training to be a pro wrestler. Both of them are indie stars, but they both grew up with a similar obsession with their training. They are currently learning organic chemistry and the psychology of tag-team wrestling. They are both eager to prove to the wrestling world that two independents can be successful when they team up.

To become a professional wrestler, it is important to learn from and practice with a variety of people and wrestle against as many different opponents as possible. Learning from and practicing with seasoned wrestlers will allow you to develop your persona and character as well as improve your style. Don't be afraid to ask them a lot of questions, as they are more than willing to impart their wisdom and tips.

Wrestling is all about entertainment, and that means teamwork is essential. The audience expects great performance, and they expect a good performance. It is important to view other wrestlers as teammates and learn how to work with them. Practice heavy-contact moves with teammates to learn how to work together. Teamwork is the most important aspect of training to become a pro wrestler. The more you work together, the better you will become at it.

How to Become a Professional Wrestler

If you have always wanted to become a professional wrestler, this article will teach you how to get into the best shape of your life and become a top-notch competitor. It'll also teach you how to select a quality wrestling school, study the works of the greats, and get in the ring. Read on to learn how to become a professional wrestler! Hopefully you'll find these tips useful.

Get in the Best Shape of Your Life

While training for wrestling, it is also a good idea to create a healthy diet and lifestyle. The right nutrition can increase your metabolism and keep you burning calories long after the workout is over. Adding a dedicated ritual to your life will make it easier to stick to your workout routine. The best way to stay on track with your nutrition is to set goals and stick to them. Keeping yourself focused and disciplined will also help you reduce temptations.

Wrestling is a great way to get into good shape. Wrestling involves multiple muscle groups, making it the perfect cardiovascular workout. It also boosts your self-confidence and mental health. Although lifting weights and running on the treadmill can improve your cardiovascular health, wrestling incorporates all muscle groups and offers a full body workout. Even if you don't have a background in wrestling, you can still get in great shape.

While training for wrestling can be a full-time job, it is important to maintain a fit lifestyle. Professional wrestlers like Shawn Michaels make it a point to stay in great shape outside the ring. Michaels used his free time between matches to stay in good shape. He has become more muscular than ever. Forget about wearing a shirt, Shawn Michaels wore a shirtless outfit at WrestleMania 32.

Wrestling is a demanding sport, and not being in excellent shape can put your career at risk. A well-rounded fitness routine will help you develop lean muscle and endurance, and you will be in the best shape of your life. You can also build your physique by developing a custom diet plan to match your goals. If you want to become a professional wrestler, you need to be in good physical shape to make it possible.

Find a Quality Wrestling School

A quality wrestling school should offer 100s of matches in front of audiences. It is not enough to say a student will get their first match. There are no shortcuts to becoming a professional wrestler. It takes time, money, and initiative to become a professional wrestler. A good wrestling school will train its students four days a week for two or three years. There are plenty of scams out there, but if you want to become a professional wrestler, you need to choose a quality wrestling school.

While the costs of a wrestling school can be expensive, there are some important aspects you should look for when choosing the right one. Most reputable schools cost between $2,500 and $5000 per year. It is best to get a quote before applying to a wrestling school, as many schools do not list their costs and only offer a quote after an applicant has registered. The next step in becoming a professional wrestler is finding a promoter. There are plenty of independent wrestling promotions online, so it is essential to search for these.

A quality wrestling school will make your life easier by providing you with good coaching. Your trainer will teach you basic wrestling techniques and tricks used by professional wrestlers. You can meet other wrestlers and network with existing ring owners. As a professional wrestler, you will also have to make a commitment to your career. Wrestling professionals suggest having a backup plan, and a backup plan if things don't work out.

A quality wrestling school will help you develop the character and charisma you need to succeed as a professional wrestler. In addition to acquiring the necessary skills to compete in professional matches, you will need to develop other important skills, such as public speaking and acting. You will also need to develop your personal character, so you must be strong and well-rounded. Your reputation and self-confidence will help you become a successful wrestler.

Study Pro Wrestling Greats

While becoming a professional wrestler requires a significant amount of training, it is possible to build a solid resume with little to no experience by studying the careers of some of the sport's greatest performers. While your first few years in the professional circuit are unlikely to be very lucrative, the vast majority of top companies require at least three years in the circuit to consider you for an open position. On your resume, you should highlight your best performances and photo opportunities. Your goal is to show a strong character, so make sure you highlight your best photo opportunities.

It is not enough to watch and study pro wrestling matches and get inspiration from them. To become a professional wrestler, you will have to spend time studying your favorite wrestlers and watching their matches. YouTube is a wonderful resource for watching professional wrestlers and learning about their career and training methods. Make it a point to attend as many events as possible and meet the people who help them achieve their dreams. Try to memorize the names of those who are influential in the sport.

Some of the best places to study the careers of the greats in the industry are Kentucky, Ohio, and Florida. Wrestling schools and training facilities in these prime locations will help you gain valuable experience and establish yourself as an exceptional wrestler. Depending on where you live, you can even get in touch with lesser promotions to get your first big fight. A strong wrestling resume will get you noticed and increase your chances of a big break.

Get in the Ring

There are several basic steps to becoming a professional wrestler. In addition to developing the skills required to wrestle, a person should get into shape and develop lean muscle. In addition, the person should develop an appropriate diet plan based on their goals. Wrestlers come in all shapes and sizes. The goal is to create a character that will appeal to the fans. While the sport can be intimidating, it is not impossible for someone with the right mindset to succeed.

Before aspiring to become a professional wrestler, you should learn as much as you can about the sport. Learn about the history of professional wrestling. Watch old matches and promos to understand what made these people popular. You should also read as many real-life stories as you can. This will give you a better idea of who each wrestler is and how to conduct yourself in the ring. To become a professional wrestler, you must be able to communicate effectively with the crowd.

In order to be a professional wrestler, you should be physically fit and in good shape. In addition to working out regularly, you should also boost your presentation skills and develop your acting skills. You can also start networking by attending wrestling shows in Florida or by contacting booking agents. Wrestlers from the WWE will give you valuable experience and help you develop your character. These contacts will prove beneficial for the career.

While it may be difficult to be a professional wrestler overnight, it's definitely possible to make it in the sport. In fact, some successful wrestlers have started from scratch and have become known for their ability to get in the ring. By working hard and taking on matches, they can build a reputation and attract promoters. As a result, they can gain national attention and eventually a full-time job.

Work on Your Character

Many professional wrestlers start their wrestling careers as amateurs, competing in local club tournaments and learning traditional wrestling techniques. Lower-level wrestling helps develop instinctive skills and character. These skills are vital to becoming a professional wrestler. Work on Your Character to Become a Professional Wrestler

Choose a character with a personality. If you like to play bad guys and bad girls, make sure to develop a character that fits your personality. You can find inspiration from comic books, anime, and even hanging out with friends and family. Whatever you choose, remember that your character is about you, not your opponent. Try to take inspiration from every possible source, and work on it to become the best.

Create a Character - Professional wrestlers have distinct personalities. For example, brawlers tend to avoid powerbombs, while high-flyers prefer submission holds. There are also combinations of different styles. Depending on your personality, you can become a heel, babyface, or a guy in between. Choose a character that will make your fan base laugh, and you'll be well on your way to becoming a professional wrestler.

Create a Unique Character - In the world of pro wrestling, a wrestler should have a unique gimmick. It's a must-have in order to make an impact and gain popularity among fans. It's also important to choose a name for your wrestler. For instance, a wrestling fanatic with a love of sports can create a character that is both sport-minded and hard-core.

How to Become a Professional Wrestler

There are different ways to make a living as a professional wrestler.

In fact, many professional wrestlers make a full-time living. Fortunately, there are some very basic steps that will get you started on your journey. Learn more about the Wrestler Job Description, how to become a professional wrestler, and how to earn a professional wrestling salary. In this article, I'll also provide you with some tips for aspiring wrestlers.

Wrestler Job Description

As a professional wrestler, you'll inevitably lose to an opponent. Losing is a tough experience, and can even damage a wrestler's self-esteem. This is where the wrestling tricks and tactics come into play. Wrestling is a competitive sport, so you'll be doing your best to avoid becoming a "real life brawler."

Steps to become a Wrestler

Regardless of your background, there are a few steps you must take to become a professional wrestler. In order to start your career as a wrestler, you must first decide what type of wrestler you want to be. This includes building up your conditioning and studying Olympic-style wrestling maneuvers. While it's not necessary to look like Batista, you should be in excellent shape. If possible, try to find a wrestling school that is run by someone in the industry. Make sure to research schools carefully before committing to one. After all, you'll need to put in some cash to learn the ropes.

Wrestling is not for everyone. You have to be strong enough to handle all of the challenges. While it may seem like a glamorous profession, it takes time, dedication, and a resilient mindset. While there are several benefits to becoming a pro wrestler, the process can be extremely challenging. To succeed in the industry, you have to have a strong mind and be willing to sacrifice everything for it.

Practice regularly. Practice wrestling against different types of wrestlers. Not only will you improve your technique, but you'll get a chance to see how other wrestlers conduct themselves. The most important tip to remember here is to always keep your character and the audience in mind. The best way to do this is to practice heavy contact moves and focus on teamwork. When you can, learn new moves to impress seasoned wrestlers.

Start looking for a wrestling school. Some wrestling schools have contacts with lesser promotions. You may find yourself getting a lot of opportunities if you join a wrestling school. With some hard work, you can make your dreams come true! Just remember that wrestling is a demanding and challenging career. As with any other job, it requires a lot of time, dedication, and a lot of effort. If you want to become a professional wrestler, you need to be in good shape and be able to train regularly.

Aside from gaining a great physique, you also have to be in great shape. To achieve this, you can hire a personal trainer or work out three to five times a week. Workouts will improve your stamina and build your muscles. You can also follow a specific diet to increase muscle mass and minimize excess fat. While training, you should also stay focused and stay mentally sharp. A healthy body is essential for a professional wrestler, so make sure you do all the necessary exercises to stay in top shape.

Professional Wrestler Salary

A professional wrestler's salary can vary considerably depending on where he or she lives. Although the national average is $58,000, professional wrestlers in sunnyvale, CA earn $72,378, and those in Santa Cruz, CA and San Rafael, CA are only slightly below. These figures reflect the average take-home pay for professional wrestlers, as each city has a different cost of living. For example, a person in Sunnyvale would need to pay $2,000 more each month to maintain the same level of living as a professional wrestler in San Francisco, CA.

In addition to a college education, you should also consider going to a professional wrestling training school. A school will give you valuable lessons from former wrestlers, as well as help you get a job with a major promotion. These schools are usually relatively expensive, ranging from $1000 to $5000 per year. Classes typically take place two to four times a week. Students should plan to spend two to three years in such a program.

Although most professional wrestlers don't use their real names, these performers are still considered some of the best athletes in the WWE. Their annual salary varies widely, but the top athletes are often paid millions of dollars per year. In fact, Brock Lesnar, John Cena, and Roman Reigns all earn over $8 million each, making their salaries comparable to those of other top stars. Those with more experience can earn $10 million or more per year as a professional wrestler.

The average professional wrestler salary in the United States is $64,168. This is the highest in the country, and the lower end of the spectrum makes up a bit less than half. According to PayScale, the salary of a professional wrestler varies considerably depending on the city and skill level. However, a professional wrestler's salary is projected to increase by 18% over the next five years. These are only a few examples of what you could expect to earn if you are interested in the sport.

While many people are interested in the glamorization of professional wrestlers on television and the Internet, the reality is that this career is difficult and demanding. Very few wrestlers become famous from top-dollar live events or TV shows, but instead they have to travel long weekends and compete in smaller events in order to get the paychecks they deserve. Besides that, most professional wrestlers make a good living in the sport, and many of these superstars have even made their money by promoting products and services.

Conclusion

There are several different ways to become a professional wrestler. While some may think that becoming a professional wrestler requires an expensive college degree, this is not always the case. You can make a full-time living while also attending school, and you can even earn extra money by working from hotels that have high-speed internet. One downside of being a professional wrestler is that it pays a low wage.

You should pursue this career choice in high school and attend a reputable wrestling school. These schools have contacts with lesser-known promotions. Even if you do not make a lot of money, attending a wrestling school is worth it. Ultimately, your dream is to become a superstar and be signed by the World Wrestling Entertainment. If you have the right attitude and drive, you can make your dreams come true!

To become a professional wrestler, you need to be in perfect physical shape and improve your presentation skills. In addition, it is essential to develop theatre and presentation skills. You must be dedicated and able to follow the code of conduct and rules of the sport. Wrestling is a separate sport from other sports, and you need to be willing to invest the time and effort necessary to become a professional wrestler.

Training is another essential part of becoming a professional wrestler. While professional wrestlers have hectic schedules, you must also be physically fit to survive the demands of the career. To be a professional wrestler, you must also be a strong athlete and maintain ample muscle mass. A wrestling career is demanding, but you can get started by taking the time to train and network. You can start today and work your way to the top by meeting other successful wrestlers.

How to Become a Professional Wrestler

If you're thinking about becoming a professional wrestler, you might be asking yourself how to get into the sport. There are many different paths that you can take, but this article will give you an idea of what's involved. We'll discuss the training necessary, and the most effective training hack. We'll also look at the real costs of becoming a professional wrestler. You may be surprised to learn that this career can cost as much as $300,000 per year.

A professional wrestler

If you want to become a professional wrestler, you will need to spend years studying the sport. There are plenty of resources online where you can watch matches from professional wrestlers. You also need to make a strong commitment to your chosen career and be prepared to make many mistakes. Many professional wrestlers have talked about the challenges of breaking into the industry and how important it is to have a backup plan in case your first professional wrestling match fails.

To become a professional wrestler, you will need to have excellent athletic skills, improve your presentation skills and develop your character in the ring. You should also attend a wrestling school to develop the skills needed to portray different characters in the sport. In addition to being in good physical condition, you will need to learn the rules of the game and adhere to a code of conduct. Wrestling is a distinct sport, and training is similar to other professional sports.

Practice your routines and move sets. While a professional wrestler might not always be in the ring, he or she should practice against different wrestlers to build his or her skill set. This way, the wrestler can learn their persona and character from watching other professional wrestlers. It is also important to practice heavy-contact moves and make sure that you learn how to work together with your teammates.

You can find a local wrestling school. The school you choose should have contacts with both the big and smaller promotions. During training, you'll also develop the contacts you need to get a job in the wrestling world. It is crucial that you attend a wrestling school that has a long list of graduates and a high quality teaching staff. Wrestling is not a career for everyone, and it requires heart and dedication to succeed. You won't be able to make much money from it, and wrestling can have negative effects on your personal life, so you will have to practice daily.

Training required to become professional wrestler

Before you can enter the world of professional wrestling, you must train like a pro. You must learn how to act, communicate effectively, and build a good reputation. You must also develop your personal character, and you must be willing to risk failure and injury in the process. As with any profession, you must not be weak. You'll be put in positions you're not capable of handling, and crowds can react very violently.

In addition to learning the basics of the sport, you should focus on developing your body. If you're not already muscular, you may need to start working out at an early age. Wrestlers must be fit and have a well-developed physique, since the sport requires a macho appearance. A bodybuilding program tailored to your body type will help you reach this goal. If you're an aspiring wrestler, make sure to follow a structured fitness regimen.

Wrestling schools are an excellent place to begin training. They will train you for four days a week, for three hours each day, and will charge you over $100 per session. If you're a teenager, try enrolling in a wrestling school in your hometown. If you're not able to attend one in your local area, you can try training with Ohio Valley Wrestling or TNA. The school also has contacts with smaller promotions.

Count the real costs of professional wrestling

If you're thinking about becoming a professional wrestler, there are many things you need to know. While wrestling can pay you upwards of $25 per show, it also requires a significant amount of cash to get started. Buying wrestling gear, attending an introductory class, and other administrative costs are just a few of the expenses you need to budget for when starting out. Fortunately, many wrestling schools offer discounts for lump sum payments and previous experience.

As a professional wrestler, you'll be paid well, but not a lot at first. While you'll be spending many hours on the road and at various events, you won't be earning very much at first. Then, you'll likely sustain minor injuries and be without benefits from a regular 9-to-5 job. To counter this, you should also budget for any travel expenses you incur while on tour.

Bonus payments are another source of income for professional wrestlers. While the amount of bonus payments is not always listed on a contract, it's important to understand that each individual wrestler earns a certain amount per show. In 2016, Triple H earned $1.65 million from his in-ring earnings. His booking contract stipulated that he would earn a base salary of $1 million, but he also received six-fifths of that amount in bonus payments. The bonuses come in several forms, including live events, royalties, and the like.

The real costs of becoming a professional wrestler vary by country. The United States' market is huge, but it's not the only country where professional wrestling is popular. In Japan, Mexico, and Central/North America, the sport is particularly popular, and it was widely watched in the U.K. for many years. The sport has also become very popular among the public, and high-profile figures in the sport have risen to become celebrities or cultural icons in their own countries.

How to Become a Professional Wrestler

If you want to become a professional wrestler, then you need to get in shape. Wrestling is one of the most dangerous sports in the world, and it involves a lot of acting. You also need to be in excellent physical condition, and if possible, take up another sport before you start training for the sport. Here are some tips on how to become a pro wrestler. To get an edge over your competitors, you should be in top physical condition and try other sports like soccer or rugby.

The Entrance

The Entrance to Professional Wrestling is a critical part of a professional wrestler's performance. It has many connotations, and it can make or break a wrestler's performance. In the case of a professional wrestler, an impressive entrance will elicit a strong response from the crowd. This is particularly true for the WWE superstars, who are in the midst of a UK arena tour.

WWE superstars have created memorable entrances by using vehicles, such as limos and motorcycles. While it may not be practical to drive down the ring in a motorbike or a Jeep, the music's hypnotic nature fits the cult-like nature of Wyatt and his Family. The music also adds an air of menace to the entrance. Fans seem to love impactful entrances.

Some entrance themes feature the voice of the wrestler - a recognizable catchphrase. Some are recorded, with the singer or wrestler delivering a motivational speech. For example, Dwyane Johnson's theme includes the words "If you can smell what the Rock is cooking!" while Booker T's famous catchphrase is "Don't hate the player, hate the game!"

Some wrestlers have unofficial entrances, such as Brian Cage and Jake Hager. A recent extension of his contract will keep him on the top of the list. While wrestling is no easy feat, a unique entrance can make a big impact. When a wrestler has a scream worthy of a movie, he'll be remembered for the rest of his life. There are many other reasons to remember Goldberg's Entrance to Professional Wrestling.

The Shine

Firstly, network. Attend as many wrestling events as you can. Wrestling shows are a hotbed of networking for professional wrestlers, so make sure you attend as many as you can. Not only will you be able to network with other wrestlers, you will be able to promote yourself as a professional wrestler. The more wrestling shows you attend, the more opportunities you will have to get booked.

Once you have a passion for the sport, the next step is to find a good mentor who has experience in the business. A mentor can help you with your training and also find promotions. Wrestling is a team sport, and every wrestler in the ring competes to entertain the crowd. If you are not ready to dedicate a large portion of your life to wrestling, you can always try your luck in Las Vegas or Louisville.

The Cut-Off

While most people think that becoming a professional wrestler is a young person's game, you can actually start as a teenager. While there are some great athletes who have been wrestling since their teens, you will be much more successful if you begin early.
To become a professional wrestler, you will need to spend a few years working for free in a minor company. It's crucial to build your name, establish your skills, and make the right friends. Wrestling is a sport of talent, and you must have the passion to excel. There are several ways to get in, including joining the training circuit with WWE or joining a country promotion such as TNA.

Firstly, you must be willing to train hard. You should prepare yourself by studying as much as possible. YouTube is a great place to get these videos. You must also be willing to take risks, including making yourself a fool. Wrestlers need to be strong and have the self-confidence to survive tough matches. If you're weak, you'll be tossed off a show. If you're not strong enough, the crowd will hate you.

The Heat

The Heat is a term used to describe the energy that is produced during a professional wrestling match. The name is a play on the word "heat." For example, X-Pac was known as the "Heat" in the WWF's Invasion storyline. The "Bossman Heat" was used at one point, but its usage declined after Ray Traylor's death.

There are two types of heat: hometown heat and regional heat. When wrestling in your hometown, fans might cheer for you more than normal, especially if you're working as a heel. However, Kurt Angle did not receive any boos in Pittsburgh. Therefore, it's important to work on developing your character and your wrestling abilities before making the move to become a superstar. If you're passionate about wrestling, you should also study the art of professional wrestling and network in your community.

If you're thinking about becoming a professional wrestler, you'll find that this profession is the perfect career choice for some people. While you can still make a living with a full-time job in the sports entertainment industry, you can also become a part of the WWE's Heat by attending training sessions and joining wrestling organizations. These programs will teach you how to become a professional wrestler.

The Comeback

We love to watch wrestlers who have been away for a long time make their big comeback, but not every comeback is a success. Many comebacks fail because the talent and writing team behind them fail to sustain the energy after the initial flurry of excitement. Here are some reasons why WWE comebacks are so unsuccessful. A successful comeback is one where the star and fans are both satisfied.

CM Punk: It is unlikely that this is the true reason why CM Punk is staging a comeback, but it is possible that the former WWE champion is planning a return. While this would be a great comeback, it is even more surprising that CM Punk is considering a comeback, given that his exit from the company was widely considered a final. Some even implied that he would never return.

The retirement

There is a reason why the WWE announces the retirement of some of its most popular superstars. Wrestlers can sustain serious injuries on the ring, including broken bones, concussions, and even paralysis. They can also be paralyzed and, in extreme cases, even die. It is important to remember that no one knows how long an athlete will be out of the ring.

Erick Stevens, the first African-American WCW champion, recently announced his retirement from professional wrestling. His career has many chapters. He was a member of the Nation of Domination stable, and he gave The Rock an opportunity to compete under him. He also formed a tag team with John Bradshaw Layfield, known as The APA. In 2010, he announced his retirement from professional wrestling.

After retiring, professional wrestlers can do many things, depending on their interests and desires. Some have saved a significant portion of their earnings and invested them in businesses or the stock market. Others simply work in other jobs. Actors and major movie stars have all made transitions from the ring to everyday life. Many former professional wrestlers go into other industries after retiring. Some become road agents and others work as managers.

How to Become a Professional Wrestler

Learning from others and wrestling against many different people will help you improve your wrestling skills and persona. It will also help you improve your character and style. Make sure you ask lots of questions to experienced wrestlers. They are usually more than willing to give you advice and share tips. Achieving success in the world of professional wrestling may be difficult, but there are many things you can do to get started. Follow these tips to become a professional wrestler and you'll soon see yourself on the road to success!

Character development

Before developing a wrestling character, it is important to have a clear idea of what your character is. Wrestlers typically fall into two categories, babyfaces and heels. There are also "guys in between," as well as the sinister Stone Cold persona. If you are unsure, you can use your experience in the wrestling world to help you develop a character that suits your needs.

While wrestling characters are ridiculous and can change from time to time, they all share the same basic traits. Developing a human character is vital for professional wrestlers, especially in today's age. It helps overcome any potential negative stigma of wrestling and gives fans something to latch on to. Wrestling is a highly competitive industry, and developing a strong character is an important part of the process. Achieving success as a professional wrestler requires you to become a person who is charismatic and believable.

Physical feats

While a wrestling career might not be a glamorous pursuit, the physical feats required to become a professional wrestler are quite impressive. In fact, an orthopedic surgeon says he holds his breath when he watches wrestlers perform their moves. More wrestlers are attempting high-risk moves that could result in broken bones, snapped necks, torn quads, and ripped off ears.

While the WWE has always had strong superstars, there are some wrestlers with a unique physical ability that make them stand out in the crowd. Wrestlers like Mark Henry have shown their strength in many competitive matches, and they can lift even a Ford Taurus. In addition to strong genetics, John Cena's ability to lift heavy objects is legendary. He once picked up Big Show and Edge in a WrestleMania match.

To become a professional wrestler, you should first join a local wrestling team or school. Then, you should start working out and taking protein supplements. You may also want to consider joining a wrestling training school. It can help you perfect your skills and develop your character. If you can develop a unique character, you can land a pro wrestling contract. While this may seem daunting at first, it will be worthwhile in the end.

Acting skills

Pro wrestling fans want to see a show that is both entertaining and dramatic, and acting skills are an essential part of a successful character. A good pair of biceps isn't enough anymore - pro wrestlers must be able to interact with fans. If you're not able to do so, you might want to reconsider your life choice. So, if you want to become a professional wrestler, you need to work on acting skills and prepare yourself for tryouts.

In addition to wrestling, you must develop acting skills and charisma. You need to be able to make your audience laugh, entertain them and be an excellent public speaker. Acting classes and community involvement can help you become a better wrestler. You will need to travel a lot and be physically fit to get to the big show. Acting classes will also help you become a better actor and performer.

Athleticism

While many people don't consider wrestling a sport, the fact is that the majority of wrestlers are extremely athletic. Wrestlers can lift and throw two hundred pound opponents, dive out of the ring, and even flip themselves to make their impacts look more devastating. While wrestling isn't an Olympic sport, it does require a high level of athleticism. Here are some of the physical attributes you need to become a professional wrestler.

A good workout routine is essential for a wrestler. It can help improve your energy levels, your sleep, and even your outlook on life. Most wrestlers also incorporate cardio workouts and weight lifting into their training sessions. Having a clearly defined goal will help limit temptations and stay on track. A diet high in nutrients and water is a vital part of athleticism. Wrestling isn't just about hitting your opponent, but also supporting your teammates.

While many athletes start out on football fields, a lot of superstars today started on a wrestling field. WWE superstars like Brock Lesnar, Kurt Angle, and Dolph Ziggler began as talented amateur wrestlers. Others, like CM Punk, Chris Jericho, and Seth Rollins, were not born to athletic backgrounds. They trained at private wrestling schools and joined indy wrestling promotions before becoming popular enough to get noticed by the WWE.

Showmanship

Becoming a professional wrestler requires determination, skill, and the will to win. While some may bash pro wrestlers, they probably wanted to be one when they were younger. If you were to tell people that they should become a pro wrestler before the season began, you would probably get the same reaction. Instead, you have to decide whether your inner child needs fulfillment more than your adult self.

Developing your personality, acting skills, and public speaking abilities is essential to become a successful professional wrestler. Wrestlers are always networking, so they need to have the right personality and charm. By participating in community events, volunteering, and taking acting classes, wrestlers can develop their personality and become a more successful wrestler. It can take years, but you can begin building your character and showmanship now.

Preparation

There are many different routes one can take to become a professional wrestler. First, one can pursue a sport wrestling career. Most professional wrestlers begin their wrestling careers in lower-level competitions, and many local clubs have training and practice sessions. Lower-level competitions will teach students basic skills and develop instinctive character. Wrestling is a sport that requires a lot of training and dedication to be successful.

In order to be a successful wrestler, you should be prepared to travel. Wrestling is a competitive field, and you won't make much money in the first few years. It typically takes three years on the circuit to get a chance to work for a top company. Make your resume look good and highlight your best shows. Include pictures of yourself in action, and highlight the things that you do best. For example, you should show the kind of character you've built over the years.

As a pro wrestler, you'll need to learn the art of entertaining an audience. In professional wrestling, you'll want to work closely with your opponents and learn how to communicate well with them. Practice hard, and don't be afraid to fail. Failure is part of the process. But it's important to learn from it and move on to the next level. You'll be glad you did.

wrestling competitions as well.

It's important to remember that a wrestling school will be expensive, so you should find one that offers a reasonable tuition. Make sure the school has a reputation for producing successful wrestlers. Also, find a wrestling promoter in your area. Independent wrestling promotions may offer more opportunities than big companies. A wrestling school will have contacts with lesser promotions in your area, including smaller promotions.

While professional wrestling is not an easy path to a career, it can be very rewarding. It takes dedication and hard work, and you'll be rewarded with fame and fortune. Wrestling is an incredibly competitive sport, so you can be sure to face a lot of rejection as a wrestler. However, don't give up. There are many opportunities for you, and it's never too early to start training for a wrestling career.

In addition to taking classes at a wrestling school, you can join a wrestling gym or club to train. Getting started is the hardest part. Even the most promising wrestlers have to bounce back from a few injuries, so a wrestling school is the first step towards a successful wrestling career. Once you've decided to pursue the career, it's time to make plans and start training.

Creating a persona

There are many benefits of creating a persona for yourself in order to get a job as a professional wrestling star. First of all, you need to be visible. That means attending professional wrestling events and social gatherings. Professional wrestlers network with each other by showing off their skills, as well as reveling in their personas in the ring. The following are just a few of these benefits.

Developing a persona is just as important as developing the right wristlocks and wristwatches. While match quality is important, it is not the end-all of the business. While a professional wrestler's ring presentation and mechanics are essential, a persona is just as important. While developing a persona for your own career in professional wrestling can help you stand out from the crowd, it is not the only factor in getting a job.

While creating a persona can make you appear more versatile, you should remember that most professional wrestlers have little or no flexibility. That's why many of the great wrestlers in the world have been known to be both heel and face. This can also cause them to be stale, especially if they're struggling to find a job. As a result, it's crucial to come up with a unique persona based on your skills and talents.

Wrestling promotions create characters for their stars based on their personalities. Examples of successful characters are the Undertaker, Mankind, and Kane. These wrestlers are recognizable to fans who watched them in action. Many of these characters have become immortal and iconic in pro wrestling history. And fans love them even more because they're based on a real person.

Finding a manager or agent

Unlike in real life, wrestling managers are not allowed to be involved in the decision-making process. The basic function of a wrestling manager is to push his or her clients. The style of the manager will depend on whether the wrestlers align themselves with a heel or a face. A heel manager may ask the wrestler to duck tougher opponents and cheat to win. A face manager might have the wrestler challenge bigger opponents, or spend the entire interview talking about how tough the wrestler was.

If you are serious about breaking into the sport, you should seek out a manager or an agent. These professionals will help you find a match and promote you. A wrestling instructor or veteran wrestler can also be a good source of information. Just be careful not to get suckered by people who want to take advantage of you. To get the attention of a manager or agent, you should post light-hearted jokes that will make your fans laugh.

The idea of working with a manager or agent is not new. Many wrestlers and managers have been working with managers for years. Some of these managers were legitimate, handling everything from bookings to travel arrangements. Some of them became champions themselves, and others made successful careers as managers. However, women were a rarity in the early days of pro wrestling, and some women became managers instead. One of the most well-known female managers was Sherri Martel, who became a manager and champion of the NWA.

Before signing with a manager or agent, most professional wrestlers first started in amateur wrestling. In addition to learning the craft, they trained at local clubs and competed. Lower level wrestling focuses on performance and traditional wrestling. It develops a person's character and instinctive skills. A manager or agent may help with the entire process of breaking into the professional wrestling business.

Making money as a professional wrestler

There are many ways to make money as a professional wrestler. If you are willing to put in a considerable amount of time and effort, you can make as much as $25 per show. You will need to find the right training facility and spend a considerable amount of money to become an effective wrestler. Here are some tips to help you get started. In addition to being physically fit, you need to learn to be strong and stamina-building.

You can earn several thousand dollars per appearance if you have the name brand value. Most wrestlers do not advertise their booking fees publicly, but some do. Ryback, for instance, reportedly earns around $4,500 to $5,000 per appearance. Other wrestlers have reported earning upwards of $300,000 per year. While the average salary of WWE main roster wrestlers is about $500,000 per year, top talent can earn a lot more. Moreover, booking fees for professional wrestling events often include lodging and airfare.

Wrestlers make millions. Some of the best-known professionals earn between $25,000 and $1 million a year. Besides regular salaries, wrestlers can also earn money through bonus payments, merchandising, and other sources. In addition to their regular paychecks, professional wrestlers can also earn money from a variety of other means, such as selling their own merchandise, putting on shows, or appearing in movies.

*DISCLAIMER

WWE is a registered trademark of World Wrestling Entertainment.
NWA is a registered trademark of National Wrestling Alliance.
TNA is a registered trademark of Total Non-Stop Action Wrestling.

This book and contents are in no way endorsed or affiliated with any of the above companies.

Printed in Great Britain
by Amazon

20123436R00031